1

Child Safety Made Simple

John Bush

Child Safety Made Simple

Contents

Contents, continued

Introduction

This book has in it the basics of child safety for parents and their children. There are no guarantees that your child will be safe in all situations they encounter. Their chances of staying safe are greatly increased if they are taught what to do and, more importantly, what not to do. Young children do not automatically know what will harm them. It is the parents duty to teach them and to show them how to stay safe.

While no one book could cover all areas and circumstances of keeping children safe, I have tried to cover some of the more important areas. The topics discussed here offer parents a basic plan for their child's safety.

The age range for this book is for young children aged 2 years old through teenagers. However, much of the information on online safety is still relevant for young adults. The only reason I made the maximum age 18 years old is that once they reach that age they will refuse to be controlled by a parents rules.

Along with keeping children safe I have included three contracts (agreements) that will, hopefully, help children and teens make good choices. The idea behind these contracts is to let children and teens know what their parents expect from them. The contracts also have consequences included in them. These help children know what to expect when they make the wrong choices in their life. I have also put a Child Identification Kit in this book that every parent needs to use. Parents should a make copy of each contract as well as the ID Kit for each child and keep them in a safe, but convenient place.

As you read this book I want you to realize that child predators are relentless in pursuing your children. There are websites where predators exchange notes on children and teens they meet online. Chances are your children have been chatting with some of these predators. The predator will try to get your child to chat in a private chatroom for many evil reasons. Some of these predators may, at some point, tell a child their gender and maybe even their age. Parents need to be aware that some of these predators may even be performing sexual acts on themselves as your children watch. They may even entice your child to do the same thing or maybe something different which will sexually excite the predator.

Parents, once you have read this book, sit down with your children and begin teaching them what you have learned. For younger children you will need to repeat your rules and guidelines to them many times so they will remember. Since young children learn best through play, find a way to make these rules a part of this playtime. As they grow older you can begin to teach them in a more serious manner the same rules.

Here's to keeping your children safe.

Parenting Survey

We are often given surveys and asked to give our feedback to business and agencies. Filling out such anonymous surveys can allow us the safety to give feedback we might not otherwise be comfortable giving. This is what makes such surveys so valid and so necessary for organizations - to hear the truth. Now the big question: how often are we as parents completely honest with ourselves, as well? What if we had to fill out a survey on our own parenting? Could we be objective with ourselves and still love ourselves? Well, let's give it a try. How about completing the survey below about yourself? You don't have to turn it in to anybody but yourself. Remember that we improve ourselves only after facing the truth upfront. The number one benefit of risking the truth with ourselves is that we become better for our children!

	Always	Most of the time	Sometimes	When I can	Never
1. I clearly communicate my needs to my child.	1	2	3	4	5
2. I tune into my child's emotional needs.	1	2	3	4	5
3. I give my child the physical affection he/she needs.	1	2	3	4	5
4. I work with my child to solve difficult issues at home.	1	2	3	4	5
5. I control my temper when angry with my child.	1	2	3	4	5
6. I am consistent in limit setting and discipline.	1	2	3	4	5
7. I follow through with my child.	1	2	3	4	5
8. I respond in a productive manner to sibling rivalry.	1	2	3	4	5
9. I actively build my child's self-image and confidence level.	1	2	3	4	5
10. I take responsibility for my own mistakes and apologize.	1	2	3	4	5
11. I avoid giving my child silent "don't" messages (ex.: Don't bother me; Don't talk so much).	1	2	3	4	5
12. I take responsibility to reduce the stress level in my home in order to make it a peaceful place.	1	2	3	4	5
13. I teach my child to respond out of love, not out of fear.	1	2	3	4	5
14. I support my child through difficult social situations.	1	2	3	4	5
15. I tell my child **"I love you"** each and every day.	1	2	3	4	5

Now the truth serum: If your child had, the opportunity (and the cognitive and emotional maturity) to answer these questions about you as his/her parent, would the answers correlate?

Celebrate your strengths and give yourself credit for doing the world's hardest job - parenting. Reflect on your weaknesses and commit to making improvements for yourself and for your child.

Child Safety at a Glance

There are probably few things more important to you than your child's health and well-being. But even though you may try your best to keep your child healthy and safe, it is not always easy to know exactly what to do - especially when your child is injured.

Children's work is their play - and play includes many fun types of activities that also put them at risk for injury, such as running, climbing, swimming, biking, and sports. Minor accidents and injuries are part of childhood and growing up. For parents and caregivers, knowing what to do when minor injuries occur is an important part of caring for a child.

To help avoid many common childhood injuries, parents and caregivers should consider learning how to care for many common childhood injuries; tell the difference between a minor problem and a true emergency and respond accordingly; learn what to keep in a first-aid kit; and complete a checklist and phone contact list for when emergencies occur.

Injury is defined as "unintentional or intentional damage to the body resulting from acute exposure to thermal, mechanical, electrical, or chemical energy or from the absence of such essentials as heat or oxygen" (National Committee for Injury Prevention and Control, 1989). Examples include damage caused by falls, motor-vehicle crashes (e.g., to pedestrians, cyclists, occupants), poisoning, suicide, fire, drowning, suffocation, and homicide. Many of these events were once considered "accidents," or random unavoidable events. Today, injury events, like diseases, are considered predictable, preventable, and controllable using a public health approach that includes surveillance, risk-factor identification, intervention development and implementation, and evaluation and dissemination.

Since 1950, injuries have replaced infectious diseases as the dominant threat to children's health. Injuries are the leading cause of the death of children, accounting for 48 percent of mortality in children one to fourteen years of age in the United States. In every industrialized country, injury is the leading killer of children, accounting for almost 40 percent of all deaths in this age group.

About twenty children die every day in the United States from a preventable injury: more than die from all other diseases combined. Motor-vehicle crashes result in the most deaths in every age bracket past age one. One in four children annually will be injured severely enough to miss school or require medical attention or bed rest, and for every injury-related death, there are approximately 19 hospitalizations, 233 hospital emergency-department visits, and 450 physician visits.

The most serious injuries to children are traumatic brain injuries and injuries from residential fires, which are particularly lethal, disabling, disfiguring, and the most costly to treat. Traumatic brain injuries account for 39 percent of all injury-related death in those under twenty years of age, or about 5,000 deaths per year in the United States. Residential fires result in about 900 deaths to this age group each year.

Can childhood injuries be prevented?

Childhood injury prevention encompasses prevention of both violence and unintentional injury. Prevention of childhood injuries has been successful due to three highly interdependent strategies: (1) education and behavior change, (2) technology and engineering, and (3) legislation and enforcement.

Education and behavior-change strategies are designed to reduce risky behaviors, provide early detection of potential harm, and eliminate exposure to environmental hazards. Efforts are usually directed to adult caregivers, parents, and the child.

Legislation and enforcement have been very effective in reducing childhood injury. Examples include legislation requiring child safety seats, child-resistant closures on medications and household cleaning agents, fire-retardant clothing, and the use of bicycle helmets.

Technology and engineering contribute to the safety of consumer goods, residential homes, neighborhoods, playgrounds, and automobiles. Better product design and performance can prevent many injuries. New products such as airbags, scooters, snowboards, and in-line skates have created new patterns of injuries, often stimulating the development of new protection technology (e.g., smart airbags, lightweight knee and elbow pads, wristguards).

The use of a combination of these and other health-promotion strategies can reduce injuries. It is not a matter of allegiance to one or another type of intervention, but the need for flexibility in combining strategies to arrive at the most effective mix.

Prevention strategies include installing and maintaining smoke alarms properly; correctly using child safety seats, booster seats, and safety belts; reducing hot-water temperatures; and installing four-sided fencing around residential pools. Improving the safety of toys, installing window guards and stair gates, increasing the use of bicycle helmets and sports protection devices, slowing traffic speeds in areas where children walk and play, and reducing bullying will all prevent injuries. Supervising children at play, training children to evacuate in a fire, building safe walking paths, enforcing child-protection laws, packaging medications in child-resistant containers, and reducing access to lethal weapons would also help reduce injuries in children. Some claim that implementing proven and effective environmental interventions alone could reduce childhood injury deaths by as much as one-third.

Child safety in your home

If you have young children living in your home or visiting your home, you need to know what to do to make it safe for them. Children are curious by nature, they will explore and plunder at any given opportunity. You want to ensure that there are no hidden dangers in your home.

The National Safe Kids Campaign reports that more than 2,400 children died in home related injuries in 1997. The main causes of injuries in the home are falls, fires and burns, drowning, suffocation and choking, poisoning, and firearms. The greatest threat is to small children, as kids get older the incidences of at-home injuries decline. About 2 million children are hurt in home related injuries each year. Many of these accidents can be easily prevented by child-proofing your home. Let's look at some of the major causes of injury to children and what parents can to do to protect their children from harm.

Falls

There are many instances in the home where a child or baby can be hurt in a fall. Children have been injured by falling off of beds or furniture, slipping on floors, falling down stairs and out of windows, and many falls occur in the bathroom.

How can you prevent falls?

1. Never leave babies or small children alone on beds, changing tables or furniture.

2. Make sure the cover is fastened securely on the high chair and always use the safety belt.

3. Many falls occur on slippery floors or rugs. If you have throw rugs in your home, make sure to secure them with a rubber mat which can be found in many department stores or home decor stores.

4. Children like to play on stairs, as a result, many home injuries occur on stairs each year. Never leave kids unattended near a stairway.

5. Always use safety gates to block off access to stairs if you have babies or toddlers in the home.

6. Keep all items picked up from the stairs. Toys and other items left on stairs cause many trip and fall accidents.

7. Never leave children unattended near open windows. Screens will not prevent a child from falling out. Keep windows closed and locked if they are within the reach of children.

8. Never leave a child of any age unattended in the bathroom. Simply trying to stand up in the bathtub could cause serious injuries. Use a slip proof bath mat to prevent slips.

Fires and burns

1. Most fires and burns occur in the kitchen. To decrease your child's chances of a burn, never allow them to play in or near the kitchen.

2. Candles have become increasing popular as home decorating items. If you have candles in your home, keep the candles and matches out of children's reach.

3. When cooking, turn the handles of your pots toward the back of the stove, so that they do not hang over the front edge where small hands can reach up and grab them.

4. Be cautious when opening the oven door that a small child is not standing nearby.

5. Install plate covers on all electrical outlets to prevent burns or electrocution.

6. Keep hot food or beverages away from the edges of the counter tops so that small children cannot reach up to pull them off.

7. Make sure that your home is properly equipped with smoke alarms.

Drowning

The majority of home drownings occur in the bathtub and in pools.

1. Never leave children unattended in the bathtub or the bathroom. Small children have even drowned in toilets.

2. If you have a pool, lake, river or body of water near your home, take extra precautions to ensure that children cannot get outside without your permission.

3. Install safety gates around pools.

Suffocation and Choking

1. Small children often put things that they find on the floor into their mouths. Keep all small items off the floor and out of a child's reach.

2. Small, hard candy is also responsible for many choking incidences. Try to refrain from giving hard candy to small children. If you do give it to them, try breaking it into bite size pieces to lessen the chance of it getting lodged in their throats.

3. Cords can easily strangle small children. Keep phone cords and cords from window blinds out of a child's reach.

Firearms

The statistics of children being killed or injured by firearms is very frightening. If you choose to keep firearms, especially hand guns in a home where children live, make sure that they are educated about its dangers.

1. Never keep a loaded gun where a child of any age, including teens, can get their hands on it.

2. Keep all guns and ammunition in separate locked cabinets. Don't store them together.

3. Have safety locks installed on any guns in your possession.

4. Almost half of all firearm injuries happen in a friend's home. Make sure your child is aware of the dangers of guns and knows to tell an adult if they see a gun or if any of their friends show them a gun.

Poisoning

Children are naturally curious and automatically put things they find into their mouths. They may easily mistake pills or insecticide tablets for candy or a poisonous liquid for juice.

To help prevent accidental poisoning:

1. Never refer to medications as "candy", children may think other medications are candy and try to sneak some when an adult is not looking

2. Ask your pharmacist to put child-resistant caps on all of your prescriptions.

3. If you carry any medications in your purse, even aspirin, never leave your purse where a small child can get into.

4. When discarding old medicine bottles, dispose of any pills or liquid left in the bottle by flushing them down the toilet or down the sink.

5. Store medicine and other poisonous substances in your top cabinets where children cannot reach them. If your children are old enough to climb onto the counters, install safety latches.

Always use extra precautions when child-proofing your home. Get down on the child's level to see what looks interesting or what they may be able to reach. Children have a way of getting into things that you might think they couldn't get into. You can never do too much child proofing: in all instances, it's better to be safe than sorry.

Playground Safety

Playgrounds and outdoor play equipment provide fun, fresh air, and exercise. But they also can pose some safety hazards.

Faulty equipment, improper surfaces, and careless behavior are just a few of the hazards of playgrounds — each year, more than 200,000 kids are treated in hospital ERs for playground-related injuries. Many of these could have been prevented with the proper supervision.

You can make the playground a place that's entertaining and safe for your kids by checking equipment for potential hazards and following some simple safety guidelines. And teaching kids how to play safely is important: If they know the rules of the playground, they're less likely to get hurt.

Adult Supervision

Parents can help prevent playground accidents by taking some precautions, ensuring that there's adult supervision at the playground, and making sure that the equipment is appropriate to a child's age and maturity level.

Adult supervision can help prevent injuries by making sure kids properly use playground equipment and don't engage in unsafe behavior around it. If an injury does occur, an adult can assist the child and administer any needed first aid right away.

Kids should always have adult supervision on the playground. Young children (and sometimes older ones) can't always gauge distances properly and aren't capable of foreseeing dangerous situations by themselves. Older kids like to test their limits on the playground, so it's important for an adult to be there to keep them in check.

Before you visit a playground, check to make sure that play areas are designed to allow an adult to clearly see kids while they're playing on all the equipment.

Playground Design Safety

The most important factors in evaluating the safety of any playground are surface, design and spacing, and equipment inspection and maintenance.

Surfaces

A proper playground surface is one of the most important factors in reducing injuries — and the severity of injuries — that occur when kids fall from equipment. The surface under the playground equipment should be soft enough and thick enough to soften the impact of a child's fall.

Here are some things to consider:

- Concrete, asphalt, and blacktop are unsafe and unacceptable. Grass, soil, and packed-earth surfaces are also unsafe because weather and wear can reduce their capacities to cushion a child's fall.

- The playground surface should be free of standing water and debris that could cause kids to trip and fall, such as rocks, tree stumps, and tree roots.

- There should be no dangerous materials, like broken glass or twisted metal.

- The surfaces may be loosely filled with materials like wood chips, mulch, sand, pea gravel, or shredded rubber.

- Surfacing mats made of safety-tested rubber or rubber-like materials are also safe.

- Rubber mats and wood chips allow the best access for people in wheelchairs.

- Loose-fill surface materials 12 inches deep should be used for equipment up to 8 feet high. The material should not be packed down because this will reduce any cushioning effect.

- No surfacing materials are considered safe if the combined height of playground and the child (standing on the highest platform) is higher than 12 feet.

- The cushioned surface should extend at least 6 feet past the equipment. Additional coverage may be needed, depending on how high a slide is or how long a swing is.

- If there is loose-fill over a hard surface (like asphalt or concrete), there should be 3-6 inches of loose-fill like gravel, a layer of geotextile cloth, a layer of loose-fill surfacing material, and then impact mats under the playground equipment.

Keep in mind that even proper surfacing can't prevent all injuries. Also, the greater the height of the equipment, the more likely kids are to get injured if they fall from it.

Design and Spacing

Playground equipment should be designed for three different age groups: infants and toddlers under 2, 2- to 5-year-olds (preschoolers), and 5- to 12-year-olds (school-age kids).

In the safest playgrounds, play areas for younger children are separated from those meant for older kids and signs clearly designate each area to prevent confusion.

Younger children should not play on equipment designed for older kids because the equipment sizes and proportions won't be right for small kids, and this can lead to injury. Likewise, older kids shouldn't play on equipment designed for younger ones. Smaller equipment and spaces can cause problems for bigger kids.

Here are some things to check for to ensure the equipment is designed and spaced to be safe:

- Guardrails and protective barriers should be in place for elevated surfaces, including platforms and ramps.

- Play structures more than 30 inches high should be spaced at least 9 feet apart.

- Swings, seesaws, and other equipment with moving parts should be located in an area separate from the rest of the playground.
- Swings should be limited to two per bay.
- Tot swings with full bucket seats should have their own bay.
- Swings should be spaced at least 24 inches apart and 30 inches between a swing and the support frame.
- Be sure there are no spaces that could trap a child's head, arm, or any other body part. All openings on equipment (for example, rungs on a ladder) should measure less than 3½ inches *or* they should be wider than 9 inches.
- Playground equipment with moving parts — like seesaws and merry-go-rounds — should be checked for pinch points that could pinch or crush a child's finger or hand.

Maintenance and Inspection

Whether your kids play on a home or public playground, it's important for you to take a general look at the equipment to make sure that it is clean and well maintained.

- There should be no broken equipment.
- Wooden equipment should not be cracking or splintering.
- Metal equipment should not be rusted.
- The fence surrounding a public playground should be in good condition to prevent kids from running into surrounding traffic.
- Surface materials on the playground should be maintained regularly so that the surfacing is loosely packed and covers all appropriate areas — especially the fall zones surrounding playground equipment.
- Playground equipment should be made of durable materials that won't fall apart or worn down too much by the weather.

Check for objects (like hardware, S-shaped hooks, bolts, and sharp or unfinished edges) that stick out on equipment and could cut a child or cause clothing to become entangled.

All hardware on equipment should be secure, with no loose or broken parts. Plastic and wood should show no signs of weakening, and there should not be any splintered or rusted surfaces.

If the local playground has a sandbox, check for hazardous debris such as sharp sticks or broken glass, and be sure that the sand is free of bugs. Sandboxes should be covered overnight to prevent contamination from animals, such as cats.

Help keep your playground clean and safe by picking up trash, using the equipment properly, and reporting any problems to the city, town, or county parks department, school, or other organization that is responsible for the upkeep of the playground. If a part seems broken, loose, or in need of other maintenance, designate it off limits immediately and report the problem to the appropriate authorities.

Teaching Kids About Playground Safety

Safe playground equipment and adult supervision are extremely important, but it's only half of the equation: Kids must know how to be safe and act responsibly at the playground.

Here are some general rules to teach your kids:

- Never push or roughhouse while on jungle gyms, slides, seesaws, swings, and other equipment.
- Use equipment properly — slide feet first, don't climb outside guardrails, no standing on swings, etc.
- If you jump off equipment, always check to make sure no other kids are in the way. When you jump, land on both feet with knees slightly bent.
- Leave bikes, backpacks, and bags away from the equipment and the area where you're playing so that no one trips over them.
- Playground equipment should never be used if it is wet because moisture causes the surface to be slippery.
- During the summertime, playground equipment can become uncomfortably or even dangerously hot, especially metal slides. So use good judgment — if the equipment feels hot to the touch, it's probably not safe or fun to play on.
- Don't wear clothes with drawstrings or other strings at the playground. Drawstrings, purses, and necklaces could get caught on equipment and accidentally strangle a child.
- Wear sunscreen when playing outside even on cloudy days so that you don't get sunburned.

Safe Equipment Guidelines

Because swings, slides, and climbing equipment are so different from one another, each requires a different set of safety considerations. And there are some kinds of equipment that are not safe for playgrounds, no matter how careful your child is.

Swing Safety

Swings are the most frequent source of childhood injuries from moving equipment on a playground. But a few simple precautions should keep kids safely swinging in the breeze:

- Swings should be made of soft material such as rubber or plastic, not wood or metal.
- Kids should always sit in the swing, not stand or kneel. They should hold on tightly with both hands while swinging, and when finished swinging, stop the swing completely before getting off.

- Children should stay a safe distance from other kids on swings, being careful not to run or walk in front of or in back of moving swings.
- Kids should never ride with more than one child to a swing. Swings are designed to safely hold only one person.

Seesaw Safety

Because seesaw use requires cooperation between kids, they're generally not recommended for preschoolers unless the seesaw has a spring-centering device to prevent abrupt contact with the ground. Regardless of design, both seesaws and merry-go-rounds should be approached with caution.

Other safety tips to keep in mind:
- Seesaw seats are like swings: one child per seat. A child who is too light to seesaw with a partner should find a different partner — not add another child to his or her side of the seesaw.
- Kids should always sit facing one another, not turned around.
- Teach kids to hold on tightly with both hands while on a seesaw, not to touch the ground or push off with their hands, and to keep feet to the sides, out from underneath the seesaw.
- Kids should stand back from a seesaw when it's in use. They should never stand beneath a raised seesaw, stand and rock in the middle, or try to climb onto it while it's in motion.

Slide Safety

Slides are safe if kids are careful when using them. Guidelines to keep in mind:
- Children should take one step at a time and hold onto the handrail when climbing the ladder to the top of the slide. They should not climb up the slide itself to get to the top.
- Kids should always slide down feet first and sitting up, never head first on their back or stomach.
- Only one child should be on the slide platform at a time, and kids shouldn't slide down in groups.
- Kids should always check that the bottom of the slide is clear before sliding down. When they reach the bottom, they should get off and move away from the end of the slide so it's clear for other kids to slide down.

Climbing Equipment Safety

Climbing equipment comes in many shapes and sizes — including rock climbing walls, arches, and vertical and horizontal ladders. It's generally more challenging for kids than other kinds of playground equipment.

Be sure your kids are aware of a safe way down in case they can't complete the climb. The highest rates of injuries on public playgrounds are associated with climbing equipment, which is dangerous if not designed or used properly. Adult supervision is especially important for younger kids.

Climbing equipment can be used safely if kids are taught to use both hands and to stay well behind the person in front of them and beware of swinging feet. When they drop from the bars, kids should be able to jump down without hitting the equipment on the way down. Remind kids to have their knees bent and land on both feet.

- Too many kids on the equipment at one time can be dangerous. Everyone should start on the same side of the equipment and move across it in the same direction.
- When climbing down, kids should watch for those climbing up; they should never race across or try to reach for bars that are too far ahead.
- Children younger than age 5 may not have the upper-body strength necessary for climbing and should only be allowed to climb on age-appropriate equipment. Preschoolers should only climb 5 feet high and school-age kids should only climb 7 feet high.

Track Ride Safety

Track rides are a form of upper-body equipment where kids hold on to a handle that slides along a track once they lift their feet. These rides require significant upper-body strength and are recommended for school-age kids and above.

- Track rides should not be included in play areas for toddlers and preschoolers.
- There should be no obstacles along the track path, especially in take-off and landing areas.
- If two track rides are next to each other, they should be spaced 4 feet apart, minimally.
- The handle should be between 64 inches and 78 inches from the surfacing.
- Nothing should be tied or attached to any part of the track ride.
- Rolling parts should be enclosed to avoid crush injuries.

Log Roll Safety

Log rolls require kids to grasp handles, then balance on top of the log as they spin it with their feet. This helps older kids to develop balance skills and increase strength.

- Log rolls are recommended for school aged-kids and above.
- All log rolls should have handholds to assist balance.
- The highest point of the log roll should be 18 inches above the protective surface.

Unsafe Playground Equipment

The following types of equipment are not safe for playgrounds:

- animal figure swings
- glider swings that hold more than one child at a time
- swinging ropes that can fray, unravel, or form a noose (any kind of rope attached to play equipment poses a strangulation hazard, so never let your child tie jump ropes or leashes onto the equipment)
- exercise rings (as used in gymnastics) and trapeze bars
- monkey bars
- trampolines

Play is an important part of kids' physical, social, intellectual, and emotional development. Following these safety tips will help your kids play as safely as possible.

School Security and Safety

Almost every week you hear news about violence in schools. You hear of kids bringing knives or guns to school. We have all heard the recent news of children walking into their school and killing students and teachers.

There are also cases of adults walking into schools, taking hostages and even killing students and teachers in their path.

"Does your school provide proper security and safety for your children?"

* Do you know what measures the school has in place to keep your child safe?
* Does the school system perform background checks before hiring new personnel?
* Does the school have security officers in the school?
* Does the school have security cameras?
* Does the school have metal detectors?
* Does the school train the faculty and staff in violence prevention?
* What are the procedures for visitors entering the school?
* Are you doing anything to make sure the school is safe for your children?

Did you know the answers to these questions? If your answer is "NO", then you need the information listed here.

Many school systems do not have the money to hire security officers or put in security cameras. They rely on students, faculty and staff to report any potentially dangerous situations. But, if the school is not training the students, faculty and staff in what to look for and how to respond, then the system will fail in keeping everyone safe.

Ask the school if they would allow you to volunteer at least part of a day to help keep an eye on things. All of the parents need to band together to become more educated with the schools security and safety policies. Schools and school systems will only change when parents become more proactive and tell them what the parents expect in school safety.

The information in this section may help you find the answers to the questions listed above.

Communicate with Your Child's School About Safety

Questions to ask your child's principal

Safety is always in season, so make sure you talk with your child's school about how they are handling this critical issue.

Ask the school principal the following questions. Then communicate your safety expectations using the sample letter below.

* Do you have a policy manual or teacher's handbook? May I have a copy or review it here?
* Is the safety of the students the first item addressed in the policy or handbook? If not, why not?
* Is the safety of students addressed at all?
* Are there policies addressing violence, weapons, drug use, sexual abuse, child-on-child sexual abuse, unauthorized visitors?
* Are background investigations performed on all staff?
* Who gathers the information?
* Who in the administration reviews the information and determines the suitability for employment?
* What are the criteria for disqualifying an applicant?
* Does the screening process apply to all employees (teachers, janitors, lunchroom staff, security personnel, part-time employees, bus drivers, etc.)?
* Is there a nurse on site at all times while children are present (including before and after school)?
* What is the nurse's education or training?
* Can my child call me at any time?
* May I visit my child at any time?
* What is your policy for when to contact parents?
* What are the parent notification procedures?
* What are the student pickup procedures?
* How is it determined that someone other than I can pick up my child?
* How does the school address special situations (custody disputes, kidnapping concerns, etc.)?
* Are older children separated from younger children during recess, lunch, rest-room breaks, etc.?
* Are acts of violence or criminality at the school documented? Are statistics maintained?
* May I review the statistics?
* What violence or criminality has occurred at the school during the last three years?
* Is there a regular briefing of teachers and administrators to discuss safety and security issues?
* Are teachers formally notified when a child with a history of serious misconduct is introduced to their class?
* What is the student-to-teacher ratio in class? During recess? During meals?
* How are students supervised during visits to the rest room?

* Will I be informed of teacher misconduct that may have an impact on the safety or well-being of my child?
* Are there security personnel on the premises?
* Are security personnel provided with written policies and guidelines?
* Is student safety the first issue addressed in the security policy and guidelines material? If not, why not?
* Is there a special background investigation conducted on security personnel, and what does it encompass?
* Is there any control over who can enter the grounds?
* If there is an emergency in a classroom, how does the teacher summon help?
* If there is an emergency on the playground, how does the teacher summon help?
* What are the policies and procedures covering emergencies (fire, civil unrest, earthquake, violent intruder, etc.)?
* How often are emergency drills performed?
* What procedures are followed when a child is injured?
* What hospital would my child be transported to in the event of a serious injury?
* Can I designate a different hospital? A specific family doctor?
* What police station responds to the school?
* Who is the school's liaison at the police department?

Characteristics of a Safe School

Research has demonstrated repeatedly that school communities can do a great deal to prevent violence. Effective prevention, intervention, and crisis response strategies operate best in school communities that:

* Focus on academic achievement.
* Promote good citizenship and character.
* Support students in making the transition to adult life and the workplace.
* Involve families in meaningful ways.
* Develop links to the community.
* Emphasize positive relationships among students and staff.
* Discuss safety issues openly.
* Help children feel safe expressing their feelings.
* Offer extended day programs for children.
* Identify problems and assess progress toward solutions.
* Treat students with equal respect.

Sample letter to send to your child's school

Dear *(Principal's name)*,

Our child, *(child's name)*, is attending your school this year. We recognize that schools face special challenges these days and we want to be certain our expectations are reasonable. If we're off base on any of these items, please let us know:

* We expect the safety of the students to be a priority;
* We expect our child to be allowed to contact us at any time she feels the need;
* We expect the school to inform us of anything that might have an impact on her safety or well-being;
* We expect the school to comply with the policies of the school district;
* We expect the school to follow all available "supplemental screening practices" set forth in the *DOJ Guidelines for the Screening of Persons Working With Children*;
* We expect the school to be a weapons-free environment;
* While we authorize you to make decisions on our behalf about educational matters, we do not authorize you to make decisions on our behalf about life-and-death matters;
* We rely upon you or your designates to notify us of any threats to commit violent acts at the school. Even if our child is not specifically named, since she could be in the environment of targeted individuals, we want to be informed so we can evaluate the risks. We request that a safety committee of parents be formed, and that the committee be notified of all threats to commit violent acts;
* *other points specific to your child*.

Just as we hold you to your duty as principal, so do we ask you to hold us to ours as parents. On this point please advise us of ways we can help you develop a safer school. Knowing that you face bureaucratic, political, and budgetary challenges, there is surely something we can do to help.

We're confident that if your office and our family work together, our child will have the best possible experience at school. At the same time, we want to assist you in furthering the well-being of all the students.

Sincerely,
(Your names)

Top 10 Lures Used by Child Predators

This section deals with child predators and some of the lures they will use to befriend a child. These 10 lures are only a few of the ways predators can get your children to trust them. The sections to follow will give you information on keeping your children safe from predators whether they are online or just at the playground.

1. The Helpless Lure: This is a person who needs help carrying boxes to his car, or to find a lost dog, or lost child.

    Prevention: Tell children that **adults don't ask kids for help** in any way. Adults should ask adults for help or directions or whatever they want.

2. The Promise Lure: This is when the predator promises to take the child to Mommy and Daddy. Or perhaps promises a surprise or candy in the car.

    Prevention: Tell children that they are **NEVER** to go with anyone unless Mom or Dad has instructed them to.

3. The Gift Giving Lure: This is the predator who gives the child candy, toys, money, or other gifts.

    Prevention: Tell children **NEVER** to accept gifts from anyone unless they received permission from Mom and Dad. This includes money from other family members (especially when the child is told to keep a secret). Tell children that we don't keep secrets in our family.

4. The Messenger: This is the predator who tells the child that "Mommy was in a car accident" and the child is to go with them. Or "Your Mom called and asked me to pick you up today."

    Prevention: Tell children the names of people you have entrusted as emergency back ups. Remind them **NEVER** to go with anyone unless Mom or Dad instructs them to.

5. The Leader (Authority Figure): This is the policeman, priest, teacher or other authority figure who uses their position and suggested authority to win the child's trust.

    Prevention: Tell children **not to go with anyone** no matter what they are wearing or who they are, even if it means that they might get into trouble. (Many authority figures tell kids they will be in trouble, or threaten to hurt Mom and Dad if the child doesn't cooperate).

6. Friendly Lure: This is the nice friendly predator who engages the child in conversation.

    Prevention: Teach children **not to talk to any adults they don't know** unless their parent is with them.

7. Playing Games: This is the predator that plays "touching games" and makes the child promise not to tell. Or other 'games' that the child feels uncomfortable with.

    Prevention: Teach children to listen to their instincts. If something makes them feel funny in their stomachs, **they are to stop, run and tell**.

8. Too Cool: This is the person who the child looks up to as "cool." Perhaps a friend's older sibling, or a relative or a neighbor who has the latest video games.

    Prevention: Teach children to listen to their instincts. If someone asks them to do something they know is wrong or feels funny, teach them to **stop, run and tell**.

9. The Magician Lure: This is the predator who seemingly magically knows the child's name or other information about the child.

    Prevention: Don't put nametags on the outside of your children's clothing, books, book bags, etc.

10. The Power Predator: This is the scary predator that just grabs the child off his/her bike and throws them into the car.

    Prevention: This is the time when a child should **fight, scream, kick, bite**. Tell children that if they are on their bikes and someone tries to take them off, they should hold the bike as hard as they can while screaming, "**You're not my Mom/Dad!**

Child Safety Tips

- One in 42 children will become lost, missing, kidnapped or run away this year.
- While stranger abduction is relatively rare, it still happens.
- Most abductions are perpetrated by someone the child knows. Child abduction is a tragedy.
- It devastates the parents, families, and touches all of us.

▪ Please read the following carefully about ways to keep our children safe ▪

1. Pay attention to where your children are at all times; don't lose sight of your child in public places.

2. Never leave children alone in cars.

3. Establish strict procedures for picking your children up at school, at a friend's, a movie, etc. Tell your children not to accept rides from people with whom you have not made previous arrangements – even if they say they are a police officer, teacher, or friend of the family.

4. Establish a family code word. Tell your children never to go with someone who does not know the code word.

5. Teach your children their full names, your full name, address, and telephone number. Teach them how to reach either you or a trusted adult, and how to call for police assistance.

6. Make sure they know how to make local and long distance telephone calls. Even a small child can be taught to dial 911 or 0 for "Operator" for help.

7. Tell your children about the abduction problem in a calm and simple way as if you were teaching any other important coping skill.

8. Listen attentively if your children talk about anyone they encounter in your absence.

9. Have photographs of your children taken four times a year (especially for pre-schoolers). Make a note of birthmarks and other distinguishing features.

10. Have fingerprints taken of your children.

11. Keep an open dialog about safety; give situational quizzes about all safety issues.

12. * Remember that child predators look like regular folks. *

Child Safety Tips: Teach Your Children

1. Never to leave the yard without permission. Very small children should play only in the backyard or in a supervised play area.

2. Not to wander off, to avoid lonely places, and not to take shortcuts through alleys or deserted areas.

3. They are safer walking or playing with friends.

4. Always to come straight home from school unless you have made other arrangements.

5. Never to enter anyone's home without your prior approval.

6. To scream, run away, and tell you or a trusted adult if anyone attempts to touch or grab them.

7. Not to give out any information on the telephone, particularly their name and address, or that they are alone.

8. Never to go anywhere with anyone who does not know the family code word.

9. To keep all doors locked and only admit authorized people into the house. No one else should be permitted to enter

10. To memorize their full names and address, including city and state.

11. To memorize their telephone number, including area code.

12. How to use the telephone to make emergency, local, and long distance calls.

13. Never to go into your home if a door is open or a window is broken.

14. How to work door and window locks.

15. How to answer the doorbell and telephone when they are home alone.

16. To run to the nearest public place, neighbor, or safe house if they feel they are being followed.

17. To tell you if someone asks them to keep a secret, offers them gifts or money, or asks to take their picture.

18. To always tell you if something happened while they were away from you that made them feel uncomfortable.

Teen Online Safety Survey

A survey questioned 500 teenagers from across the United States, ages 14 to 18, about their computer habits. Listed below are the results of this survey. The answers given to these questions are disturbing.

As a parent it is your responsibility to oversee what your children do. You need to know where they go, just in case something happens. Most important of all, who they are going to see. That should be a no brainer, but many parents do not know enough about their children.

I hope these results will open your eyes to the possible dangers awaiting your children online.

Results of the survey:

Question 1: Have you ever met someone online via e-mail, instant messenger, chat room, etc.?

RESPONSE	MALE	FEMALE
Yes	71%	76%
No	29%	24%

Question 2: How often would you say you talk to people via the Internet that you don't know, but have met online?

RESPONSE	MALE	FEMALE
All the time	24%	32%
Very often	18%	19%
Sometimes	26%	26%
Not very often	26%	21%
Not at all	6%	3%

Question 3: Has anyone you have met online ever asked to meet you in person?

RESPONSE	MALE	FEMALE
Yes	63%	65%
No	37%	35%

Question 4: Have you ever had a scary online experience, or an online experience that has made you feel uncomfortable in any way?

RESPONSE	MALE	FEMALE
Yes	32%	29%
No	68%	71%

Question 5: You mentioned that you had an online experience that made you uncomfortable. Did you tell anyone about it?

RESPONSE	MALE	FEMALE
Yes	61%	61%
No	39%	39%

Question 6: Have you ever done anything online that you *would not* want your parents to know about?

RESPONSE	MALE	FEMALE
Yes	50%	59%
No	50%	41%

Question 7: Do you talk about yourself or personal things online?

RESPONSE	MALE	FEMALE
Yes	51%	58%
No	49%	42%

Question 8: Do you think your parents know what you're really doing when you're on the computer?

RESPONSE	MALE	FEMALE
Yes	53%	46%
No	47%	54%

Question 9: Do you think your parents would mind if they knew what you were really doing on the computer?

RESPONSE	MALE	FEMALE
Yes	48%	46%
No	52%	54%

Question 10: Do you think you use the computer responsibly?

RESPONSE	MALE	FEMALE
Yes	92%	90%
No	8%	10%

Question 11: Would you say that most people your age use the computer responsibly?

RESPONSE	MALE	FEMALE
Yes	39%	42%
No	61%	58%

Do some of the responses surprise you? I believe that questions ten and eleven tell the real story. The same teenagers, whose answers to some of the questions were not too bad, thought while they used the computer responsibly said they think others their age do not use the computer responsibly.

Is this a double standard? Probably not. I think they honestly believe they do act responsibly when using the computer. The real issue is how can they make that judgment if no one has ever taught them how to act when using the computer. If the same survey were given to the same teenagers after they were given an online safety course, I think the results might be different.

The bottom line is we expect children and teenagers to behave themselves, but we have not given them enough training to make reasonable judgments. Plenty of time is spent *telling* them they can't do something and not enough time *teaching* them the right things to do.

So, which are you? A *teacher* or a *teller*.

Keeping Your Child Safe from Online Predators

--- Every child, if they spend much time on the internet, has been touched by an online predator and doesn't know it.

--- While the computer age has opened a whole new world for our children to explore and learn from, the "information superhighway" also has a dark side we all need to be aware of. Just as they prey on land, Pedophiles lurk on the Internet waiting to lure innocent children into their web of deviance, looking for their next victim.

--- These deviates meet others who claim children for their victims, share stories, pictures and encourage each other along the way. The tricks they use on the Internet are a little different. They can hide behind the screen. No one can tell if they are 12, 20, 40, or any age. They know how to relate to children and find it easy to communicate on that level. They present themselves in areas children frequent and pose as children.

--- They get to know the child they are communicating with and pass themselves off as a friend. Often, they will use smoking cigarettes, using drugs, talking about sex, or some activity they should not be involved with as an incitement to lure the child to meet them without anyone knowing. The trap is then laid. An adult will lure the child out to meet with them. Thinking it's another child, they set off to meet their friend.

--- What happens next depends on the plan of the predator. For some, this would be enough. The fact that they won their trust enough to get them to meet them may be all the ground rules they need to molest the child. Some may attempt a closer relationship by playing the con a little longer.

--- The key to all of this is that child predators are cons. Their goals are as varied as their egos. The limits for one may just be the beginning point for another. There is no way to predict how any given predator will react.

--- Their personalities differ. Their needs are not the same in many ways. There is only one thing they have completely in common. That is the fact that they find their thrill in luring a child into their well concocted plan.

Your Child and Online Predators

- Using Internet communication tools such as chat rooms, e-mail, and instant messaging can put children at potential risk of encountering online predators.

- The anonymity of the Internet means that trust and intimacy can develop quickly online. Predators take advantage of this anonymity to build online relationships with inexperienced young people.

- Parents can help protect their kids by becoming aware of the risks related to online communication and being involved in their kids' Internet activities.

How do online predators work?

1. Predators establish contact with kids through conversations in chat rooms, instant messaging, e-mail, or discussion boards. Many teens use peer support online forums to deal with their problems. Predators often go to these online areas to look for vulnerable victims.

2. Online predators try to gradually seduce their targets through attention, affection, kindness, and even gifts, and often devote considerable time, money, and energy to this effort.

3. They are aware of the latest music and hobbies likely to interest kids.

4. They listen to and sympathize with kids' problems.

5. They also try to ease young people's inhibitions by gradually introducing sexual content into their conversations or by showing them sexually explicit material.

6. Some predators work faster than others, engaging in sexually explicit conversations immediately. This more direct approach may include harassment or stalking.

7. Predators may also evaluate the kids they meet online for future face-to face contact.

Which young people are at risk?

Young adolescents are the most vulnerable age group and are at high risk of being approached by online predators. Young adolescents are exploring their sexuality, moving away from parental control, and looking for new relationships outside the family. Under the guise of anonymity, they are more likely to take risks online without fully understanding the possible implications.

Young people who are most vulnerable to online predators tend to be:

1. new to online activity and unfamiliar with netiquette

2. aggressive computer users

3. the type to try new, edgy activities in life

4. actively seeking attention or affection

5. rebellious

6. isolated or lonely

7. curious

8. confused regarding sexual identity

9. easily tricked by adults

10. attracted by subcultures apart from their parents' world

▪ **Kids feel they are aware of the dangers of predators, but in reality, they are quite naive about online relationships**.

How can parents minimize the risk of a child becoming a victim?

1. Talk to your kids about sexual predators and potential online dangers.

2. Young children should not use chat rooms—the dangers are too great. As children get older, direct them towards well-monitored kids' chat rooms. Encourage even your teens to use monitored chat rooms.

3. If your children take part in chat rooms, make sure you know which ones they visit and with whom they talk. Monitor the chat areas yourself to see what kind of conversations take place.

4. Instruct your children to never leave the chat room's public area. Many chat rooms offer private areas where users can have one-on-one chats with other users chat monitors cannot read these conversations.

*These are often referred to as "**whisper**" areas.*

5. Keep the Internet-connected computer in a common area of the house, never in a child's bedroom. It is much more difficult for a predator to establish a relationship with your child if the computer screen is easily visible. Even when the computer is in a public area of your home, sit with your child when they are online.

6. When your children are young, they should share the family e-mail address rather than have their own e-mail accounts. As they get older you can ask your Internet Service Provider (ISP) to set up a separate e-mail address, but your children's mail can still reside in your account.

7. Tell your children to never respond to instant messaging or e-mails from strangers. If your children use computers in places outside your supervision—public library, school, or friends' homes—find out what computer safeguards are used.

8. If all precautions fail and your kids do meet an online predator, do not blame them. The offender always bears full responsibility. Take decisive action to stop your child from any further contact with this person.

How can your kids reduce the risk of being victimized?

There are a number of precautions that kids can take, including:

1. Never downloading images from an unknown source - they could be sexually explicit.

2. Using e-mail filters.

3. Telling an adult immediately if anything that happens online makes them feel uncomfortable or frightened.

4. Choosing a gender-neutral screen name that does not contain sexually suggestive words or reveal personal information.

5. Never revealing personal information about themselves (including age and gender) or information about their family to anyone online and not filling out online personal profiles.

6. Stopping any e-mail communication, instant messaging conversations, or chats if anyone starts to ask questions that are too personal or sexually suggestive.

7. Posting the family online agreement near the computer to remind them to protect their privacy on the Internet.

How can you tell if your child is being targeted?

It is possible that your child is the target of an online predator if:

1. Your child or teen spends a great deal of time online. Most children who are victims of online predators spend a lot of time online, particularly in chat rooms, and may close the doors to their rooms and be secretive about what they do when they go work on their computer.

2. You find pornography on the family computer. Predators often use pornography to sexually victimize children—supplying things such as Web sites, photos, and sexual e-mail messages as a way to open sexual discussions with potential victims. Predators may use photos of child pornography to convince a child that it is normal for adults to have sex with children. You should be aware that your child may hide pornographic files on disks, especially if other family members use the computer.

3. Your child or teen receives phone calls from people you do not know, or makes calls (sometimes long distance) to numbers you do not recognize.

After establishing contact with your child online, some online predators may try to contact young people to engage in phone sex, or to try to set up a real-world, face-to-face meeting.

If children hesitate at giving out their home phone number, online sex offenders will provide theirs. Some even have toll-free 1-800 numbers, so potential victims can call them without their parents' knowledge.

Others will tell children to call collect—and then, with Caller ID or Call Display, the predators can easily determine the child's phone number.

Do not allow your child to meet a stranger they have met online, in person, without your supervision.

4. Your child or teen receives mail, gifts, or packages from someone you don't know. It's common for offenders to send letters, photographs, and gifts to potential victims. Online sex offenders even send airline tickets to entice a child or teen to meet them in person.

5. Your child or teen withdraws from family and friends, or quickly turns the computer monitor off or changes the screen if an adult enters the room. Online predators work hard to drive wedges between kids and their families, often exaggerating minor problems at home. Sexually victimized children tend to become withdrawn and depressed.

6. Your child is using someone else's online account. Even kids who don't have access to the Internet at home may meet an offender while online at a friend's house or at another public place, even the library. Predators sometimes provide victims with a computer account so they can communicate.

What can you do if your child is being targeted?

• If your child receives sexually explicit photos from an online correspondent, or if she or he is solicited sexually in e-mail, instant messaging, or some other way online, contact your local police. Save any documentation including e-mail addresses, Web site addresses, and chat logs to share with the police.

• Check your computer for pornographic files or any type of sexual communication—these are often warning signs.

• Monitor your child's access to all live electronic communications, such as chat rooms, instant messaging, and e-mail. Online predators usually meet potential victims in chat rooms at first, and then continue communicating with them through e-mail or instant messaging.

Internet Filter Resources

Bsafe Online http://www.bsafehome.com	FilterPak http://www.surfguardian.net
Computer Cop http://www.computercop.com	Internet Guardian http://www.internet-guardian.com
ContentProtect http://www.contentwatch.com	Netmop http://www.netmop.com
CyberPatrol http://www.cyberpatrol.com	Net Nanny http://www.netnanny.com
Cyber Sentinel http://www.securitysoft.com	Parental Guidance http://www.parentalguidance.org/
Cybersitter http://www.cybersitter.com	Safe2Read http://www.safe2read.com
Cyber Snoop http://www.pearlsw.com	Software 4 Parents http://www.software4parents.com
	Trustworthy Communication, LLC. http://www.kidmail.com

Sex Offender Registries

Listed below are a few websites that list sex offenders. Not all sex offenders may be listed on every site. We advise you to look through each one.

Find Local Sex Offenders
Search over 400,000 known sex offenders free. Updated daily.
http://www.childsafenetwork.org

Sexual Predator Search
Map of your area, Names, Addresses, Pictures, Offenses & E-mail Alerts.
http://www.NationalAlertRegistry.com

Sex Offenders Near You?
Search Registered Offenders Free. Free Child ID Kit Too. We care!
http://www.FreeSexOffendersSearch.org

National Sex Offenders Registry - Registered Sex Offenders List
Registered sex offenders list the national sex offenders registry. Access information on 491,720 registered sex offenders. Do sex offenders live in your neighborhood?
http://www.registeredoffenderslist.org/

STOP Sex Offenders! | National Sex Offender Registry Main Page
Your source for child and family safety information; National Sex Offender Registry; Free Child ID System & more!
http://www.stopsexoffenders.com/statelistings.shtml

National Registry Alert / Predator Report
Search for or be alerted to, all registered sex offenders living in or moving into your area using National Alert Registry. We offer detailed maps and ...
http://www.recordsearch-usa.com/

Parent's Guide to Online Slang

This page is important for parents, because your child may be using these abbreviations, acronyms, initials and slangs while online. Parents need to print out this entire page, so you can understand what your child is saying when they talk online. Too many parents **"ASSUME"** their child is being good while surfing the net. Well, guess what? All children need their parents to supervise their lives.

If you don't know what your child does online, **OR** where they go online, **OR** what they say to others, **OR**, most importantly, who they talk with; then you, as a parent, are inviting a sexual predator to invade your child's life. Save your child's life by letting them know you know what they do and say while on the Internet.

*NOTE: The information and list below is from **http://www.safersurfers.org/**. We recommend every parent go to this site and search every page. They offer information to keep children safe by showing parents what to look for.

Kids and **teens** love to **chat** in their own **secret language** on their **computers**. **Online**, they enter **chat rooms**, **send email** and **instant messages** using a series of **acronyms**, **initials**, **letters**, and **secret words** on the **Internet**. **Internet slang** has become widely used. These **acronyms** and their **secret meanings** are listed below so that you can **interpret** the **words** and what they **mean**.

The following is a list of email, instant message and chatroom acronyms (slang) and word abbreviations commonly used online - and their meanings:

A	
AAMOF	as a matter of fact
ABFL	a big fat lady
ABT	about
ADN	any day now
AFAIC	as far as I'm concerned
AFAICT	as far as I can tell
AFAICS	as far as I can see
AFAIK	as far as I know
AFAYC	as far as you're concerned
AFK	away from keyboard
AISI	as I see it
AIUI	as I understand it
AKA	also known as
AML	all my love
ANFSCD	and now for something completely different
AOHe**	Derogatory term for America Online (AOL)
ASAP	as soon as possible
ASL	assistant section leader
ASL	age, sex, location
ASLP	age, sex, location, picture
A/S/L	age/sex/location
ASOP	assistant system operator
ATM	at this moment
AWA	as well as
AWHFY	are we having fun yet?
AWGTHTGTTA	are we going to have to go trough this again?
AWOL	absent without leave
AWOL	away without leave
AYOR	at your own risk

AYPI?	and your point is?
B	
B4	before
B4N	bye for now
BAC	back at computer
BAG	busting a gut
BAK	back at the keyboard
BBIAB	be back in a bit
BBL	be back later
BBLBNTSBO...	be back later but not to soon because of...
BBR	burnt beyond repair
BBS	be back soon
BBS	bulletin board system
BC	be cool
B/C	because
BCnU	be seeing you
BEG	big evil grin
BF	boyfriend
B/F	boyfriend
BFN	bye for now
BG	big grin
BION	believe it or not
BIOYIOB	blow it out your I/O port
BITMT	but in the meantime
BM	bite me
BMB	bite my bum
BMTIPG	brilliant minds think in parallel gutters
BKA	better known as
BL	belly laughing
BOB	back off bastard
BOL	be on later
BOM	bitch of mine
BOT	back on topic
BRB	be right back
BRBB	be right back *****
BRBS	be right back soon
BRH	be right here
BRS	big red switch
BS	big smile
BS	bull ****
BSF	but seriously folks
BST	but seriously though
BTA	but then again
BTAIM	be that as it may
BTDT	been there done that
BTOBD	be there or be dead
BTOBS	be there or be square
BTSOOM	beats the **** out of me
BTW	by the way
BUDWEISER	because you deserve what every individual should ever receive
BWQ	buzz word quotient

BWTHDIK	but what the heck do I know
BYOB	bring your own bottle
BYOH	Bat You Onna Head
B&	Banned
C	
C&G	chuckle and grin
CAD	ctrl-alt-delete
CADET	can't add, doesn't even try
CDIWY	couldn't do it without you
CFV	call for votes
CFS	care for secret?
CFY	calling for you
CID	crying in disgrace
CLM	career limiting move
CM@TW	catch me at the web
CMIIW	correct me if I'm wrong
CNP	continue in next post
CO	conference
CRAFT	can't remember a ******* thing
CRS	can't remember ****
CSG	chuckle snicker grin
CTS	changing the subject
CU	see you
CU2	see you too
CUL	see you later
CUL8R	see you later
CWOT	complete waste of time
CWYL	chat with you later
CYA	see ya
CYA	cover your ***
CYAL8R	see ya later
CYO	see you online
D	
DBA	doing business as
DCed	disconnected
DFLA	disenhanced four-letter acronym
DH	darling husband
DIIK	darn if i know
DGA	digital guardian angel
DGARA	don't give a rats ***
DIKU	do I know you?
DIRTFT	do it right the first time
DITYID	did I tell you I'm distressed
DIY	do it yourself
DL	download
DL	dead link
DLTBBB	don't let the bed bugs bite
DMMGH	don't make me get hostile
DQMOT	don't quote me on this
DND	do not disturb
DTC	darn this computer

DTRT	do the right thing
DUCT	did you see that?
DWAI	don't worry about it
DWIM	do what I mean
DWIMC	do what I mean, correctly
DWISNWID	do what I say, not what I do
DYJHIW	don't you just hate it when...
DYK	do you know
E	
EAK	eating at keyboard
EIE	enough is enough
EG	evil grin
EMFBI	excuse me for butting in
EMFJI	excuse me for jumping in
EMSG	email message
EOD	end of discussion
EOF	end of file
EOL	end of lecture
EOM	end of message
EOS	end of story
EOT	end of thread
ETLA	extended three letter acronym
EYC	excitable, yet calm
F	
F	female
F/F	face to face
F2F	face to face
FAQ	frequently asked questions
FAWC	for anyone who cares
FBOW	for better or worse
FBTW	fine, be that way
FCFS	first come, first served
FCOL	for crying out loud
FIFO	first in, first out
FISH	first in, still here
FLA	four-letter acronym
FOAD	**** off and die
FOAF	friend of a friend
FOB	**** off *****
FOC	free of charge
FOCL	falling of chair laughing
FOFL	falling on the floor laughing
FOS	freedom of speech
FOTCL	falling of the chair laughing
FTF	face to face
FTTT	from time to time
FU	****** up
FUBAR	****** up beyond all recognition
FUDFUCT	fear, uncertainty and doubt
FUCT	failed under continuous testing
FURTB	full up ready to burst (about hard disk drives)

FW	freeware
FWIW	for what it's worth
FYA	for your amusement
FYEO	for your eyes only
FYE	for your entertainment
FYEO	for your eyes only
FYI	for your information
G	
G	grin
G2B	going to bed
G&BIT	grin & bear it
G2G	got to go
G2GGS2D	got to go get something to drink
G2GTAC	got to go take a crap
G2GTAP	got to go take a pee
GA	go ahead
GA	good afternoon
GAFIA	get away from it all
GAL	get a life
GAS	greetings and salutations
GBH	great big hug
GBH&K	great big huh and kisses
GBR	garbled beyond recovery
GBY	god bless you
GD&H	grinning, ducking and hiding
GD&R	grinning, ducking and running
GD&RAFAP	grinning, ducking and running as fast as possible
GD&REF&F	grinning, ducking and running even further and faster
GD&RF	grinning, ducking and running fast
GD&RVF	grinning, ducking and running very
GD&W	grin, duck and wave
GDW	grin, duck and wave
GE	good evening
GF	girlfriend
GFETE	grinning from ear to ear
GFN	gone for now
GFU	good for you
GG	good game
GGU2	good game you too
GIGO	garbage in garbage out
GJ	good job
GL	good luck
GL&GH	good luck and good hunting
GM	good morning / good move / good match
GMAB	give me a break
GMAO	giggling my *** off
GMBO	giggling my butt off
GNBLFY	got nothing but love for you
GMTA	great minds think alike
GN	good night
GOK	god only knows

GOWI	get on with it
GPF	general protection fault
GR8	great
GR&D	grinning, running and ducking
GtG	got to go
GTSY	glad to see you
H	
H	hug
H/O	hold on
H&K	hug and kiss
HAK	hug and kiss
HAGD	have a good day
HAGN	have a good night
HAGS	have a good summer
HAG1	have a good one
HAHA	having a heart attack
HAND	have a nice day
HB	hug back
HB	hurry back
HDYWTDT	how do you work this darn thing
HF	have fun
HH	holding hands
HHIS	hanging head in shame
HHJK	ha ha, just kidding
HHOJ	ha ha, only joking
HHOK	ha ha, only kidding
HHOS	ha ha, only seriously
HIH	hope it helps
HILIACACLO	help I lapsed into a coma and can't log off
HIWTH	hate it when that happens
HLM	he loves me
HMS	home made smiley
HMS	hanging myself
HMT	here's my try
HMWK	homework
HOAS	hold on a second
HSIK	how should i know
HTH	hope this helps
HTHBE	hope this has been enlightening
HYLMS	hate you like my sister
I	
IAAA	I am an accountant
IAAL	I am a lawyer
IAC	in any case
IC	I see
IAE	in any event
IAG	it's all good
IAG	I am gay
IAIM	in an Irish minute
IANAA	I am not an accountant
IANAL	I am not a lawyer

IBN	I'm buck naked
ICOCBW	I could of course be wrong
IDC	I don't care
IDGI	I don't get it
IDGARA	I don't give a rat's ***
IDGW	in a good way
IDI	I doubt it
IDK	I don't know
IDTT	I'll drink to that
IFVB	I feel very bad
IGP	I gotta pee
IGTP	I get the point
IHTFP	I hate this ******* place
IHTFP	I have truly found paradise
IHU	I hate you
IHY	I hate you
II	I'm impressed
IIT	I'm impressed too
IIR	if I recall
IIRC	if I recall correctly
IJWTK	I just want to know
IJWTS	I just want to say
IK	I know
IKWUM	I know what you mean
ILBCNU	I'll be seeing you
ILU	I love you
ILY	I love you
ILYFAE	I love you forever and ever
IMAO	in my arrogant opinion
IMFAO	in my ******* arrogant opinion
IMBO	in my bloody opinion
IMCO	in my considered opinion
IME	in my experience
IMHO	in my humble opinion
IMNSHO	in my, not so humble opinion
IMO	in my opinion
IMOBO	in my own biased opinion
IMPOV	in my point of view
IMP	I might be pregnant
INAL	I'm not a lawyer
INPO	in no particular order
IOIT	I'm on Irish Time
IOW	in other words
IRL	in real life
IRMFI	I reply merely for information
IRSTBO	it really sucks the big one
IS	I'm sorry
ISTM	it seems to me
ISTR	I seem to recall
ISWYM	I see what you mean
ITFA	in the final analysis

ITRO	in the reality of
ITRW	in the real world
ITSFWI	if the shoe fits, wear it
IVL	in virtual live
IWALY	I will always love you
IWBNI	it would be nice if
IYKWIM	if you know what I mean
IYSWIM	if you see what I mean
J	
JAM	just a minute
JAS	just a second
JASE	just another system error
JAWS	just another windows shell
JIC	just in case
JJWY	just joking with you
JK	just kidding
J/K	just kidding
JMHO	just my humble opinion
JMO	just my opinion
JP	just playing
J/P	just playing
JTLYK	just to let you know
JW	just wondering
K	
K	OK
K	kiss
KHYF	know how you feel
KB	kiss back
KISS	keep it simple sister
KIS(S)	keep it simple (stupid)
KISS	keeping it sweetly simple
KIT	keep in touch
KMA	kiss my ass
KMB	kiss my butt
KMSMA	kiss my shiny metal ass
KOTC	kiss on the cheek
KOTL	kiss on the lips
KPC	keeping parents clueless
KUTGW	keep up the good work
KWIM	know what I mean?
L	
L	laugh
L8R	later
L8R G8R	later gator
LAB	life's a *****
LAM	leave a message
LBR	little boys room
LD	long distance
LG	lovely greetings
LGR	little girls room
LHM	Lord help me

LHU	Lord help us
LL&P	live long & prosper
LNK	love and kisses
LMA	leave me alone
LMABO	laughing my *** back on
LMAO	laughing my *** off
MBO	laughing my butt off
LMHO	laughing my head off
LMIRL	let's meet in real life
LMFAO	laughing my fat *** off
LMK	let me know
LOL	laughing out loud
LOL	lots of love
LOL	lots of luck
LOLA	laughing out loud again
LOML	light of my life (or love of my life)
LOMLILY	light of my life, I love you
LOOL	laughing out outrageously loud
LSHIPMP	laughing so hard I peed my pants
LSHMBB	laughing so hard my belly is bouncing
LSHMBH	laughing so hard my belly hurts
LTNS	long time no see
LTR	long term relationship
LTS	laughing to self
LULAS	love you like a sister
LUWAMH	love you with all my heart
LY	love ya
LYK	let you know
LYL	love ya lots
LYLAB	love ya like a brother
LYLAS	love ya like a sister
M	
M	male
MB	maybe
MILF	mother I'd like to ****
MYOB	mind your own business
MWBRL	More Will Be Revealed Later
M8	mate
N	
N	in
N2M	not too much
N/C	not cool
NALOPKT	not a lot of people know that
NE1	anyone
NETUA	nobody ever tells us anything
NFI	no ******* idea
NIFOC	Nude In Front Of Computer
NL	not likely
NM	never mind / nothing much
N/M	never mind / nothing much
NMH	not much here

NMJC		nothing much, just chillin'
NOM		no offense meant
NOTTOMH		not of the top of my mind
NOYB		none of your business
NOYFB		none of your ******* business
NP		no problem
NTA		non-technical acronym
N/S		no ****
NVM		nevermind
	O	
OBTW		oh, by the way
OIC		oh, I see
OF		on fire
OFIS		on floor with stitches
OK		abbreviation of oll korrect (all correct)
OL		old lady (wife, girlfriend)
OLL		on-line love
OM		old man (husband, boyfriend)
OMG		oh my god / gosh / goodness
OOC		out of character
OT		Off topic / other topic
OTOH		on the other hand
OTP		on the phone
OTTOMH		off the top of my head
	P	
PAW		parents are watching
PDS		please don't shoot
PDOMA		pulled directly out of my ***
PEBCAK		problem exists between chair and keyboard
PLZ		please
PM		private message
PMJI		pardon my jumping in (Another way for PMFJI)
PMFJI		pardon me for jumping in
PMP		peed my pants
POAHF		put on a happy face
POOF		I have left the chat
POTB		pats on the back
POS		parents over shoulder
POTS		parents over the shoulder - (My parents are watching, I can't really talk)
PPL		people
PS		post script
PSA		public show of affection
	Q	
Q4U		question for you
QSL		reply
QSO		conversation
QT		cutie
	R	
RAT		remote(ly) activated Trojan
RCed		reconnected
RE		hi again (same as re's)

ROFL	rolling on floor laughing
ROFLAPMP	rolling on floor laughing and peed my pants
ROFLMAO	rolling on floor laughing my *** off
ROFLOLAY	rolling on floor laughing out loud at you
ROFLOLTSDMC	rolling on floor laughing out loud tears streaming down my cheeks
ROFLOLWTIME	rolling on floor laughing out loud with tears in my eyes
ROFLOLUTS	rolling on floor laughing out loud unable to speak
ROTFL	rolling on the floor laughing
RTF	read the FAQ
RTF	read the FAQ
RTM	read the manual
RTSM	read the stupid manual
RUMOF	are you male or female
RUTTM	are you talking to me
RUUP4IT	are you up for it?
RVD	really very dumb
S	
S2R	send to receive
SAMAGAL	stop annoying me and get a live
SCNR	sorry, could not resist
SETE	smiling ear to ear
SH	so hot
SH	same here
SHICPMP	so happy I could pee my pants
SHID	slaps head in disgust
SHMILY	see how much I love you
SNAFU	situation normal, all ****** up
SO	significant other
SOHF	sense of humor failure
SOMY	sick of me yet?
SPAM	stupid persons' advertisement
SRY	sorry
SSDD	same **** different day
STBY	sucks to be you
STFU	shut the **** up
STW	search the web
SWAK	sealed with a kiss
SWALK	sweet, with all love, kisses
SWL	screaming with laughter
SIM	sh*t, it's Monday
SITWB	sorry, in the wrong box
S/U	shut up
SYS	see you soon
SYSOP	system operator
T	
TA	thanks again
TCO	taken care of
TGIF	thank god its Friday
THTH	to hot to handle
THX	thanks
TIA	thanks in advance

TIIC	the idiots in charge
TJM	that's just me
TLA	three-letter acronym
TMA	take my advice
TMI	to much information
TMS	to much showing
TNSTAAFL	there's no such thing as a free lunch
TNX	thanks
TOH	to other half
TOY	thinking of you
TPTB	the powers that be
TSDMC	tears streaming down my cheeks
TT2T	to tired to talk
TTFN	ta ta for now
TTT	thought that, too
TTUL	talk to you later
TTYIAM	talk to you in a minute
TTYL	talk to you later
TTYLMF	talk to you later my friend
TU	thank you
TWMA	till we meet again
TX	thanx
TY	thank you
TYVM	thank you very much
U	
U2	you too
UAPITA	you're a pain in the ***
UR	your
UW	you're welcome
URAQT!	you are a cutie!
V	
VBG	very big grin
VBS	very big smile
W	
W8	wait
W8AM	wait a minute
WAY	what about you
WAY	who are you
WB	welcome back
WBS	write back soon
WDHLM	why doesn't he love me
WDYWTTA	What Do You Want To Talk About
WE	whatever
W/E	whatever
WFM	works for me
WNDITWB	we never did it this way before
WP	wrong person
WRT	with respect to
WTF	what/who the ****?
WTG	way to go
WTGP	want to go private?

WTH	what/who the heck?
WTMI	way to much information
WU	what's up?
WUD	what's up dog?
WUF	where are you from?
WUWT	whats up with that
WYCM?	will you call me?
WYMM	will you marry me?
WYRN	What's Your Real Name?
WYSIWYG	what you see is what you get
X	
XTLA	extended three letter acronym
Y	
Y	why?
Y2K	you're too kind
YATB	you are the best
YBS	you'll be sorry
YG	young gentleman
YHBBYBD	you'd have better bet your bottom dollar
YKYWTKM	you know you want to kiss me
YL	young lady
YL	you 'll live
YM	you mean
YM	young man
YMMD	you've made my day
YMMV	your mileage may vary
YVM	you're very welcome
YW	you're welcome
YWIA	you're welcome in advance
YWTHM	you want to hug me
YWTLM	you want to love me
YWTKM	you want to kiss me
YOYO	you're on your own
YY4U	two wise for you
Z	
ZZZ	sleeping, bored, tired
More	
?	huh?
?4U	question for you
>U	screw you!
/myB	kick my butt
2U2	to you too
2MFM	to much for me
4AYN	for all you know
4COL	for crying out loud
4SALE	for sale
4U	for you
=w=	whatever
G	giggle or grin
H	hug

K	kiss
S	smile
T	tickle
W	wink

Follow these links for more information on slang:

http://www.safersurfers.org/
Safe Internet Surfing

http://www.directory.google.com/Top/Computers/Internet/Chat/Guides/
Google's Index of Internet Chat Guides

http://www.ocf.berkeley.edu/~wrader/slang/a.html
A comprehensive dictionary of online slang from Berkeley

Child Identification Kit

Attach Most Recent Photo

*Please remember to update
every 4-6 months*

Place your child's hair sample here. Include 25 to 50 strands with root attached. Collect them using a clean hairbrush. Seal them in a plastic bag and tape them here.

Identifying Material

First Name: _____

Middle Name: _____

Last Name: _____

Nickname(s): _____

Current Address: _____

City, State, Zip: _____

Home Phone Number: _____

Alternative Phone Number: _____

Date of Birth _____ Gender: _____

Ethnicity: _____

Height: _____ Weight: _____

Hair Color: _____ Eye Color: _____

Other Recognizable Characteristics: _____

_____

_____

(Example - glasses, birthmarks, etc.)

Medical Information

Allergies: _____

Ongoing Medications: _____

_____

Blood Type: _____

Other Disease or Illness: _____

_____

Child Identification Kit

Fingerprint Sample

Fingerprints remain one of a parent's best resources for helping authorities identify their child. As long as the child's fingers remain unaltered by scars or other unnatural obstructions, regardless of age, fingerprint patterns will stay the same.

Follow our easy-to-use instructions for fingerprinting your child below.

Instructions for receiving the best results:

1) Use high quality stock paper or cardboard

2) Practice on scrap pieces of paper

3) Hold child's finger and guide them through the process

4) Lightly press down on ink pad or strip

5) Gently press the top of their finger down on the corresponding finger chart.
*Note: often parents try to help their children roll their fingers. However, understand that the most important aspect of the fingerprint is that it is clear and not smudged.

6) Allow fingerprints to dry in a safe place.

Left Thumb	Left Index	Left Middle	Left Ring	Left Pinky

Right Thumb	Right Index	Right Middle	Right Ring	Right Pinky

Online Code-of-Conduct Contract

1. **I will** talk with my parents to learn the rules for using the Internet, including where I can go, what I can do, when I can go online, and how long I can be online (_____ minutes or _____ hours).

2. **I will** not visit sexually explicit, or otherwise inappropriate Web sites or chat rooms, and agree to have my chat room conversations monitored.

3. **I will** never give out personal information such as my home address, telephone number, my parents' work address or telephone number, credit card numbers, or the name and location of my school without my parents' permission.

4. **I will** always tell my parents immediately if I see or receive anything on the Internet that makes me feel uncomfortable or threatened, including e-mail messages, Web sites, or even anything in the regular mail from Internet friends.

5. **I will** automatically delete any email from persons I don't know.

6. **I will** never agree to a face-to-face meeting or telephone conversation with anyone I "meet" online without first obtaining parental permission and I agree to be chaperoned if permission is granted.

7. **I will** not respond to online messages that make me feel uncomfortable and will show such messages to my parents.

8. **I will** never send pictures of myself or other family members to other people through the Internet or regular mail without first checking with my parents.

9. **I will** never download anyone else's picture or photographs without first obtaining parental permission.

10. **I will** not create a personal Web site without first obtaining parental permission. I agree to parental review of anything I want to post.

11. **I will** never give out my Internet passwords to anyone (even my best friends) other than my parents.

12. **I will** be good while online and not do anything that could hurt or anger other people or that is against the law.

13. **I will** not fill out any online surveys or register at any Web sites without first obtaining parental permission.

14. **I will** never download, install, or copy anything from disks or the Internet without proper permission.

15. **I will** never do anything on the Internet that costs money without first asking permission from my parents.

16. **I will** help my parents understand how to have fun and learn things online and teach them things about the Internet, computers and other technology.

17. **I will** let my parents know my Internet logon and chat names, listed below:

_____

_____

_____

_____

18. **I will** follow all the above rules while on any computer, e.g., at home, at a friend's house, at school, at the library, etc.

I agree to all of the above rules. I understand that breaking even one of the above rules will result in loss of Internet privileges, as well as other consequences.

Name (child) _____ Date _____

Parent or guardian _____ Date _____

Safe Driving Contract (Agreement)

For the teen-ager:

I (_____) do agree to the stipulations stated below regarding the privilege of driving a vehicle (whether it be my own, a friend's, a relative's, and/or my parents' vehicle(s)). If, at any time, I violate any part of said "Driving Contract," my driving privileges will be forfeited for a period of time as determined by law enforcement and/or by my parent(s)/guardian(s) signing below.

I will take and pass an appropriate driver-training course.

Before leaving on any driving trip, I will discuss with my parent(s)/guardian(s) where I am going and when I will be back.

I understand that my driving safely is not just protection for me, but also for every passenger in my car, and for everyone else on the road, including small children and babies on the sidewalks and in other vehicles. I understand that it is my responsibility to protect everyone. I understand that if I do not take driving seriously, I run the risk of seriously injuring or killing an innocent person or myself.

I will not speed -- particularly in school zones and/or in bad weather -- and I will obey all traffic laws (including curfews or other laws specific to my city or state). I will drive safely and defensively at all times, and I will not be a passenger in a vehicle that is being driven unsafely or illegally.

I will call -- at any time of the day or night -- a parent/guardian/friend/relative/law enforcement officer/taxi driver for help in getting home if -- for any reason -- I am not able to drive both safely and legally. The person called will come and get me immediately. If I call a taxi and cannot pay for it, my parent/guardian will pay for it. Making this intelligent and responsible phone call will NOT result in the loss of driving privileges or other punishment.

I know that the parent(s)/guardian(s) signing below will always love me and accept me -- even if I make a mistake. I also recognize that this love and acceptance requires one or both of them to suspend my driving privileges if either feel it is warranted.

I accept that the parent(s)/guardian(s) signing below have more experience than I do on the road, and so I will listen to and carefully consider the advice that I am given. If the parent(s)/guardian(s) signing below feel that more training on my part is required, I will immediately obtain more training.

I agree to pay the full cost of any traffic violation tickets, as well as the difference in the insurance premium for as long as the premium is in effect.

I agree to pay the full cost of all damages incurred that are not covered by insurance, as well as the difference in insurance premiums caused by the damages.

I will never consume alcohol, drugs or inhalants before driving or while driving -- nor will there be open containers of alcoholic beverages (mine or anyone else's), drugs or drug paraphernalia at any time in the vehicle.

I will not drive anyone else's vehicle, nor allow anyone to drive my vehicle, unless I have prior permission from my parents, or unless it is an emergency involving illness or injury. I will not loan my vehicle to any other person, unless I have prior permission from my parents.

I will never allow anyone who has been consuming alcoholic beverages, drugs or inhalants to drive a vehicle in which I am a passenger.

I will always drive with my seat belt properly and securely fastened. I will never transport more passengers than I have seat belts. All seat belts will be in working order. All passengers will wear a seat belt, and all seat belts will be fastened properly and securely before the vehicle moves. If anyone refuses to buckle up, or unbuckles while I am driving, I will stop the vehicle.

I will keep all vehicles I drive clean, inside and out, and in good working order. I will not be a driver or passenger in a vehicle that is not safely maintained. I will wash and wax the vehicle _____ times per month, and I will not bring my parent's vehicle(s) home without at least a half of a tank of gas.

I will not behave rudely in my vehicle or with my vehicle -- to other passengers, other drivers, law enforcement, or the parent(s)/guardian(s) signing below.

I will keep my eyes on the road at all times, and -- while driving -- *I will not use my cell phone*, change a CD, light a cigarette, read a map, put on makeup, fish in my purse, glove compartment or wallet (or engage in any other behavior not specified here that prevents me from devoting my full attention to the road).

Note: Studies have proven that no one is a safe driver while talking or texting on a cell phone. This rule should apply to both teens and adults.

I recognize that driving a vehicle is a privilege, not a right, and I also recognize that each parent/guardian signing below has individual veto power over my driving privileges for the duration of my life as a minor.

For the parent(s)/guardian(s):

I/We (_____) do grant (_____)
access to a vehicle as long as he/she obeys all stipulations noted above.

I/We agree to pick up (_____) at any time, from any
place, if he/she is ever in a situation where he/she or another driver has consumed
alcohol, inhalants, drugs or other illegal or inappropriate substance.

In order to set a good example, I/We agree to also obey all stipulations as noted above.
(You might wish to add a consequence for the parents as well if rules are broken).

I/We have read the above agreement and agree to the stipulations.

Signed on this Date: _____

_____ Teen-ager

_____ Parent and/or Guardian

_____ Parent and/or Guardian

Home Rules Contract

for

_____ **Family**

(last name of family)

All family members, whose signatures are present on this document below, are in agreement with and will follow the rules and consequences of this Home Rules Contract as listed:

1. (list rule) _____

Consequence: _____

_____

Privilege: _____

_____

2. (list rule) _____

Consequence: _____

_____

Privilege: _____

_____

3. (list rule) _____

Consequence: _____

_____

Privilege: _____

_____

4. (list rule) _____

Consequence: _____

_____

Privilege: _____

_____

5. (list rule) _____

Consequence: _____

_____

Privilege: _____

_____

Signatures of family members *(contract must be signed by all family members involved in contract)*

Caregivers

Other Caregivers

* _____
  Parent

* _____
  Grandparent #1

* _____
  Parent

* _____
  Grandparent #2

* _____
  Step Parent

* _____
  Other Caregiver #1

* _____
  Step Parent

* _____
  Other Caregiver #2

Teens/Preteens

* _____
   Teen/child #1

* _____
   Teen/child #2

* _____
   Teen/child #3

* _____
   Teen/child #4

* _____
   Teen/child #5

* _____
   Teen/child #6

Closing Comments

The information in this book has been put together to help parents keep their children safe.

The information in this book is only a basic starting place. I urge parents to do more research to continue to find ways of keeping their children safe. The more you as parents know the better you can arm your children against harm.

Since you have taken the time to read this book, I hope you will share this information with other parents.

I have put together a Child Safety Seminar on CD ROM that is easy to present to a group. This is a Power Point presentation that has all the material to present the seminar. Go to my website at http://www.A-Better-Child.org if you are interested in this CD.

We must all stop sexual predators from harming children.

Thank you,
John Bush

For more on child safety, visit our website: http://www.A-Better-Child.org.

Here are some of the topics on our website:

Are You Setting a Good Example?	Good Study Habits
Autism: The Facts and Symptoms	Grandparents Role in the Family
Avoiding Divorce	Helping Children Deal with Death
Being Bullied by a Teacher?	Helping Families Survive Divorce
"Bullies" - How To Stop Them?	Home Schooling Information
Building a Christian Family	How do online predators work?
Building Family Strengths	How To Choose a Babysitter
Child Abuse Statistics	Insight for Single Parents
Child Safety: Kidnappers & Molesters	Keeping Your Romance Alive
Children and ADD/ADHD	Kids Fun Sites
Children and Alcoholism	Learning Good Manners & Etiquette
Children and Depression	Mom, Dad, I'm Pregnant!
Children and Drugs	Mothers are Special People
Children and Eating Disorders	Overcoming Peer Pressure
Children and Sex Abuse	Parenting Survey
Children Dealing with Terminal Illness	Parenting Tips
Children's Online Safety	Parent's Guide to Online Slang
Children's Poetry Websites	Playing Games with Your Children
College Preparation/ACT/PSAT/SAT	Preventing Child Suicide
Cooking With Your Children	Reading With Your Children
Dangers of Myspace	School Security and Safety
Dissociative Identity Disorder (MPD)	Sex Offender Registries
Do Your Kids Enjoy Doing Chores?	Sibling Rivalry and Abuse
Family Communication	Talking To Your Kids About Sex
Fathers' Role in Parenting	Teen Online Safety Survey
Finding Quality Family Time	Teens and Safe Driving
Free Child ID & DNA Kit	Tips for Step Parents and Step Children

www.ingramcontent.com/pod-product-compliance
Lightning Source LLC
Chambersburg PA
CBHW060206060326
40690CB00018B/4281